60

1954 – 2014

Sixty Lyric Moments

Sixty Lyric Moments was produced to commemorate
the sixtieth anniversary of Lyric Opera of Chicago.

Compiled by Roger Pines
Edited by Maggie Berndt, Holly Gilson,
Magda Krance, Lisa Middleton, Dan Novak
Stefany Phillips, and Roger Pines
Designed by Hal Kugeler
Production managed by Jocelyn Park

COVER
*Lyric began in 1954 with two "calling-card"
performances of Mozart's* Don Giovanni *with
a star-studded cast, headed by Nicola Rossi-Lemeni
in the title role.*

BACK COVER
Robert Falls's new production of Don Giovanni,
*conducted by Sir Andrew Davis and with Mariusz
Kwiecień in the title role, opened Lyric's 60th
season in 2014.*

What you hold in your hands represents the living, breathing force that is Lyric Opera of Chicago. We are delighted to invite you to explore, or perhaps experience again, some of the moments in our 60-year history that make Lyric part of Chicago's cultural essence.

We open and close these pages with *Don Giovanni*. It was the work that introduced this company to Chicago in 1954. Today it is the work that signals entry into our seventh decade with tremendous energy and ambition for the future.

Anthony Freud

All of us who love our art form have favorite repertoire and artists. We hope that you will find many of those memories represented here. At the same time, the images have been selected to showcase elements and events beyond the main stage. These are the unique moments in time that have forged Lyric's personality as a multi-dimensional arts organization, dedicated to providing a broad, deep, and relevant cultural service to Chicago and the nation.

Kenneth G. Pigott

Please join us as we celebrate our rich history, and as we strive to become the great North American opera company for the 21st century through our commitment to our core values of excellence, relevance, and fiscal responsibility.

We are confident that with you, Lyric will remain a company in which opera, the most incomparably passionate and exciting of all art forms, can continue to illuminate our hearts and minds, and can forge a real, lasting connection with our audiences.

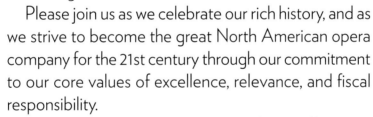

Anthony Freud
General Director

Kenneth G. Pigott
President

Lyric Opera Presidents

Carol Fox
1954 – 1955

Thomas I. Underwood
1956 – 1957

Leonard Spacek
1957 – 1958

Alfred C. Stepan, Jr.
1959 – 1961

J. W. Van Gorkom
1962 – 1963

Daggett Harvey
1964 – 1968

Edward F. Blettner
1969 – 1971

T. M. Thompson
1972 – 1975

William S. North
1976

William O. Beers
1977 – 1979

Archie R. Boe
1980 – 1982

Angelo R. Arena
1983

William B. Graham
1984 – 1991

James W. Cozad
1992 – 1995

Edgar D. Jannotta
1996 – 2000

Allan B. Muchin
2001 – 2006

Richard P. Kiphart
2007 – 2011

Kenneth G. Pigott
2012 –

Dates reflect fiscal years.

1

1954
*The elegant Lyric audience
arrives for opening night.*

2

1954
Lyric's first full season (eight operas, sixteen performances) opens with Norma, *starring Maria Callas in her American debut.*

1954
*Tito Gobbi (unofficial "godfather" of Lyric Opera)
sings his first Lyric performance of his signature
role, Scarpia in Tosca, a portrayal reprised in seven
subsequent seasons.*

4

1955
*Maria Callas sings her only
staged performances of the title
role of* Madama Butterfly.

5

1956
*Lyric presents the American debut of
Bruno Bartoletti (Lyric Opera's future artistic
director), who conducts* Il trovatore.

From morning to night I have my running shoes on. I used to think I was quite an athlete in my day — a great hockey player, a basketball player. I used to play tennis. And I still can run — and I run most of the days and the nights.

— *Carol Fox*

6

1956
Lyric Theatre of Chicago is renamed Lyric Opera of Chicago, with Carol Fox as general manager.

1958
The first Lyric radio broadcast, on WBBM-AM & FM: opening night of Falstaff *with, left to right, Anna Maria Canali (Meg Page), Renata Tebaldi (Alice Ford), Tullio Serafin (conductor), Alvinio Misciano (Fenton), and Tito Gobbi (title role).*

1961
Lyric's first world premiere: Vittorio Giannini's
The Harvest, *the first Lyric production under*
a Ford Foundation program for the promotion
of American opera. Left to right, Geraint Evans
(Lem), Barry Morell (Mark), Marilyn Horne
(Lora), and William Wildermann (Sam).

8

9

1962
*Rudolf Nureyev makes his American debut as principal male dancer
in Lyric's only production to date of Borodin's* Prince Igor. *Pictured,
left to right, are Boris Christoff (Konchak), Sonia Arova (prima ballerina),
Rudolf Nureyev, and Oskar Danon (conductor).*

1964
*Bruno Bartoletti and Pino Donati
(pictured with Carol Fox) are named
co-artistic directors of Lyric Opera.*

10

11

1965

Lyric stages the first Chicago performances of Berg's Wozzeck. *Geraint Evans (right) sings the title role, with Paul Gudas (left) as a Soldier.*

12

1970
Lyric presents the American professional stage premiere of Britten's Billy Budd, *with Theodor Uppman (right of center) in the title role.*

1971

WFMT inaugurates its broadcasts of Lyric opening nights with Rossini's Semiramide, *starring Joan Sutherland (left) in the title role and Marilyn Horne (right) as Arsace. The program wins a Peabody Award.*

13

14

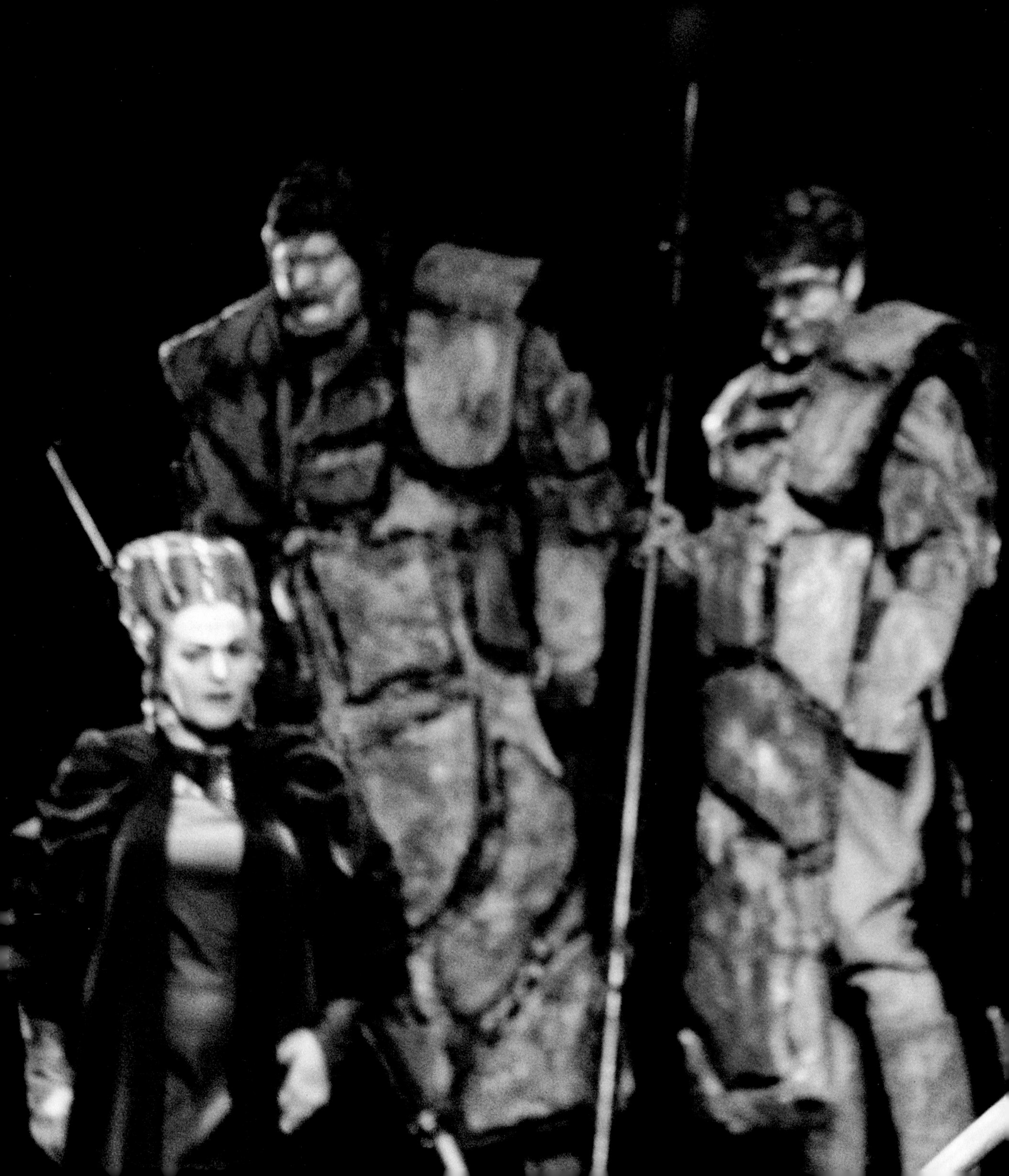

1971
Das Rheingold, *first of the four operas in Wagner's* Ring *cycle, premieres at Lyric (one Ring opera is presented per season through 1974). Pictured, left to right, are Grace Hoffman (Fricka), Bengt Rundgren (Fasolt), Hans Sotin (Fafner), and Hubert Hoffmann (Wotan).*

1972
Lyric premieres Pier Luigi Pizzi's production of La bohème, *the most often-performed production in Lyric history (six revivals, most recently in 2007–08).*

15

16

America's first internationally celebrated ballet star, Maria Tallchief, former prima ballerina of New York City Ballet, is named Lyric's ballet director; she creates and oversees the company's new ballet corps.

1974

The company's professional-development program, Lyric Opera School of Chicago, is incorporated; renamed Lyric Opera Center for American Artists in 1981; known since 2006 as The Patrick G. and Shirley W. Ryan Opera Center. Pictured is the LOCAA production of Rossini's La cambiale di matrimonio, *presented as* The I. O. U. Wedding, *1996. Left to right: Patricia Risley, Mark McCrory, Franco Pomponi, Jeffrey Ray.*

1975
*Bruno Bartoletti is named
sole artistic director, following
the death of Pino Donati.*

20

1978

The world premiere of Krzysztof Penderecki's Paradise Lost, *followed by performances at La Scala and for Pope John Paul II (Act Two only) in Rome. Left to right: William Stone (Adam), Peter van Ginkel (Satan), and Ellen Shade (Eve).*

1978
*Broadway's Harold Prince makes his operatic
debut directing a new production of* La fanciulla
del West, *starring Carol Neblett (Minnie),
Carlo Cossutta (Dick Johnson),
and Gianpiero Mastromei (Jack Rance).*

1979
Lyric presents a star-studded 25th-anniversary gala, hosted by Tito Gobbi and Sam Wanamaker. Pictured backstage are, left to right, Leontyne Price, Luciano Pavarotti, Carol Fox, and Mirella Freni. Special guests included Elisabeth Schwarzkopf, Eleanor Steber, Giulietta Simionato, Giuseppe di Stefano, and Nicola Rossi-Lemeni.

22

23

opera**thon**
93

Sponsored by American Airlines

Be Bullish on Lyric Opera of Chicago!
Tune into our fundraising marathon!

October 30
WFMT 98.7 FM

bullish
on LYRIC
opera
CHICAGO

Order today by mail or phone **312.267.6767** or pledge your support during operathon 93 October 30 WFMT 98.7 fm 7 am to midnight **312.565.0300** or **1 800.USA.WFMT**

OPERA**THON**

"TWO THUMBS UP!"
for
LYRIC OPERA OF CHICAGO

OCTOBER 5
WFMT 98.7 FM

PRE-ORDER TODAY BY MAIL or FAX 312-332-0304
on OCTOBER 5, call toll-free 888-726-5700 7am to Midnight
Sponsored by **AmericanAirlines**®

A Project of the Lyric Opera Chapters

1979

Lyric's first Operathon. Over the years, many celebrities appear on Operathon catalogue covers, including Michael Jordan, Gene Siskel and Roger Ebert, Ann Landers, John Mahoney, Mike Ditka, Bono, and others, as well as international opera stars including Renée Fleming, Joyce DiDonato, Susan Graham, Plácido Domingo, Luciano Pavarotti, Samuel Ramey, and many more.

our fundraising marathon!

Pre-order today
by mail or fax

On September 27,
phone toll-free
1-888-726-5700,
8 AM to Midnight

A Project of the
Lyric Opera Chapters

Lyric Operathon
16 Oct 2010

LIVE COVERAGE ON
98.7WFMT

BONO / ROCK STAR & HUMANITARIAN

OPERATHON 2001
GREAT **PREMIUMS!** GREAT **ENTERTAINMENT!**
ALWAYS BEST OF SHOW **13 OCTOBER** WFMT **98.7**

PICTURED JOHN MAHONEY, SUBSCRIBER, AND EDDIE

SPONSORED BY **AmericanAirlines** AND **ERNST & YOUNG**

25

1981
With the retirement of Carol Fox, Ardis Krainik becomes general manager (the title changes to general director beginning with the 1987–88 season).

1983

Peter Sellars makes his Lyric debut as director of The Mikado *(company premiere, new production), concluding the company's three-season series of spring operettas sponsored by the City of Chicago. Pictured at center are Dan Sullivan (Pish-Tush) and Neil Rosenshein (Nanki-Poo).*

26

27

1983
Lyric stages the company premiere of Shostakovich's
Lady Macbeth of Mtsensk, *conducted by Bruno Bartoletti*
and directed by Liviu Ciulei, with Marilyn Zschau in
the title role.

*PBS telecasts the company premiere
of Tchaikovsky's* Eugene Onegin, *starring
Wolfgang Brendel and Mirella Freni.
It is later released on commercial video.*

28

1984
Lyric's Marilyn Horne Festival includes a concert performance of Handel's Rinaldo (with Mario Bernardi conducting), an aria concert (with Leonard Slatkin conducting), and a solo recital (with pianist Martin Katz, pictured).

29

We treat our artists with consideration and love.
That's the operative word at Lyric Opera — we love
each other and work in a harmonious surrounding,
and that's how you put on the best music.

— *Ardis Krainik*

1985–86
*Projected English titles are introduced at Lyric for
the company premiere of Puccini's* La rondine.

30

31

1986-87
August Everding's production of Die Zauberflöte *proves a huge hit in its Lyric premiere and returns in five different seasons, most recently 2011-12. (Pictured are Lauren McNeese, Meredith Arwady, and Erica Strauss as the Three Ladies and Michael Schade as Tamino in the 2005-06 revival.)*

32

1986–87

Lyric inaugurates a Composer-in-Residence program to create operas performed by the Lyric Opera Center for American Artists. The program continues through the 2002-03 season (sponsored by Brena and Lee Freeman, Sr.). Pictured are scenes from, left to right, William Neil's The Guilt of Lillian Sloan, *Bruce Saylor's* Orpheus Descending, *Shulamit Ran's* Between Two Worlds (The Dybbuk), *and Michael John LaChiusa's* Lovers and Friends (Chautauqua Variations).

33

1987–88
*Lyric Opera's Women's Board
produces its first wine auction.*

1989–90
To open the 35th anniversary season, Madison
Street Bridge in downtown Chicago is renamed
"Lyric Opera Bridge" by Mayor Eugene Sawyer,
pictured with Ardis Krainik.

34

35

1990–91
Lyric launches its "Toward the 21st Century" artistic initiative, funded by the National Endowment for the Arts, to present two 20th-century works each season, one European and one American. The latter begins with Dominick Argento's The Voyage of Edgar Allan Poe, *pictured here.*

36

1992–93
The world premiere of a Lyric commission:
William Bolcom's McTeague, directed by Robert
Altman. Pictured are Catherine Malfitano (Trina)
and Ben Heppner (title role).

1993–94
*The Lyric debut of Renée Fleming, opposite
Samuel Ramey, in the company premiere
of Carlisle Floyd's* Susannah.

1993–96
Lyric becomes the new owner of the Civic Opera House, marking the first time the theater, built in 1929, has actually been owned by a resident Chicago opera company. With its $50-million portion of the Facilities Fund, Lyric launches a $100-million capital campaign, Building on Greatness: An Opera House for the 21st Century, *to finance the purchase and renovation.*

39

40 **1997**
*William Mason becomes general director
following the death of Ardis Krainik.*

1997–98
The world premiere of Anthony Davis's Amistad, directed by George C. Wolfe, starring Mark S. Doss (Cinque), Thomas Young (The Trickster), and Florence Quivar (Goddess of the Waters).

1999-2000

The world premiere of a Lyric commission:
William Bolcom's A View from the Bridge,
directed by Frank Galati, the final work in
the "Toward the 21st Century" artistic initiative.

At left, composer William Bolcom, librettist
Arnold Weinstein, and playwright Arthur Miller.

At right, cast members Mark McCrory (Marco),
Catherine Malfitano (Beatrice), Juliana Rambaldi
(Catherine), Kim Josephson (Eddie), and
Gregory Turay (Rodolpho).

43

1999–2000
Matthew A. Epstein, a longtime Lyric artistic consultant, is appointed artistic director. Left to right: Sir Andrew Davis, William Mason, Bruno Bartoletti, Matthew A. Epstein.

2000–01
*Lyric Opera presents its first-ever free
pre-season outdoor concert at Grant Park.
Approximately 20,000 people attend.*

44

45

2000–01
Sir Andrew Davis begins his tenure as Lyric's first music director and principal conductor; he opens the season with the Lyric premiere of Tchaikovsky's The Queen of Spades.

2002–03
The company premiere of Sweeney Todd (the first musical to be part of a mainstage season) stars Bryn Terfel in the title role and Judith Christin as Mrs. Lovett.

47

2004–05

The 50th-anniversary season opens with a new production of Don Giovanni. Bryn Terfel (center) is surrounded by (left to right) Ildebrando D'Arcangelo, Kyle Ketelsen, Isabel Bayrakdarian, Kurt Strait, Karita Mattila, and Susan Graham. Left: Bryn Terfel (title role) and Isabel Bayrakdarian (Zerlina).

2004

The 50th anniversary gala, with many of the world's most celebrated stars onstage. Fundraising breaks all Lyric records for a single event. After the gala, four generations of renowned mezzo-sopranos: left to right, Frederica von Stade, Marilyn Horne, Giulietta Simionato, and Susan Graham. Below, the Lyric Opera Chorus and Lyric Jubilarians.

48

2004–05
The world premiere of a Lyric commission:
William Bolcom's A Wedding *features an all-star*
cast headed by Jerry Hadley, Lauren Flanigan,
Catherine Malfitano, and Mark Delavan.

49

We're not curing cancer, but we are
presenting some of the greatest works
conceived by some of the greatest
creative artists of the past 400 years.

— *William Mason*

50

2006–07

On opening night of the season, William Mason announces that the Lyric Opera Center for American Artists will henceforth be known as The Patrick G. and Shirley W. Ryan Opera Center at Lyric Opera of Chicago. Mr. and Mrs. Ryan are pictured with the 2008-09 Ensemble and Gianna Rolandi (seated left), director of the Ryan Opera Center from 2006 to 2013.

2010
Renée Fleming is appointed as Lyric Opera's first creative consultant. She is pictured (top) at the 2014 Merit School of Music gala; with dancer Damian Woetzel and students at Manuel Perez Jr. Elementary School; and in a Q&A session with tenor Jonas Kaufmann.

51

52

2011
Anthony Freud begins his tenure as general director on October 1.

53

2012–13
The season opens with Sir David McVicar's new production of Elektra, conducted by Sir Andrew Davis, with the Lyric debut of Christine Goerke in the title role (right, with Emily Magee as Chrysothemis).

54

2012–13
Lyric's first production specifically created for family audiences, Popcorn and Pasquale, is also the first production of Lyric Unlimited, the company's new community-engagement initiative. Above: actors Nathan Randall (left) and Ross Lehman (right). Below: Ildebrando D'Arcangelo (seated left) in the title role, with Marlis Petersen as Norina (foreground, right of center) and René Barbera as Ernesto (far right).

2012–13
The gala performance of The Second City Guide to the Opera *is a Lyric Unlimited event at the Civic Opera House, co-hosted by Renée Fleming and Sir Patrick Stewart (pictured with Second City actresss Carisa Barecca).*

2012–13
The launch of Lyric's American Musical Theater Initiative with Gary Griffin's new production Oklahoma! by Rodgers and Hammerstein. Pictured below are the male chorus with Paula Scrofano (far left) as Aunt Eller and Curtis Holbrook (center) as Will Parker; and, left, Ashley Brown (Laurey) and John Cudia (Curly).

57

2012–13
Chicago's first mariachi opera — Cruzar la Cara de la Luna, *with music by José "Pepe" Martínez and libretto by Leonard Foglia — is performed at the Civic Opera House, preceding community performances in Pilsen and Waukegan. Pictured are Mariachi Vargas de Tecalitlán with Cecilia Duarte (Renata) and Octavio Moreno (Laurentino).*

58

2013–14

Lyric premiere of Dvořák's Rusalka in a new production, conducted by Sir Andrew Davis, directed by Sir David McVicar, with Ana María Martínez in the title role.

2013–14

A new production of Rodgers and Hammerstein's The Sound of Music, *starring Billy Zane (Captain von Trapp), Jenn Gambatese (Maria), and Christine Brewer (Mother Abbess), is the top-selling production in Lyric history with 71,074 tickets sold.*

59

Lyric is a real company — an organic, living organism with a sense of common purpose, collective pride, and shared ambition. It's so much more than a group of people who happen to work together.

— *Anthony Freud*

60

2014–15
The season opens with Robert Falls's new production of
Don Giovanni, *conducted by Sir Andrew Davis. The cast
includes Mariusz Kwiecień (title role), Marina Rebeka (Donna
Anna), Ana María Martínez (Donna Elvira), Kyle Ketelsen
(Leporello), Antonio Poli (Don Ottavio), Andriana Chuchman
(Zerlina), Michael Sumuel (Masetto), and Andrea Silvestrelli
(Commendatore).*

Lyric, as a major opera company, has
a dual core purpose: to provide a broad,
deep and relevant cultural service to
Chicago, and to advance the development
of our art form.

We must be a resource for our city,
stimulating creativity and cultural
awareness, attracting inward investment,
and enhancing Chicago's global reputation
as an international metropolitan center
of great renown.

Our vision is to be the great North
American opera company for the
twenty-first century, recognized globally
for our world-class artistic excellence
and innovation.

— *Anthony Freud*